Our Words Are Powerful: Our Ancestors Speak Through Us

Words To Power

Our Words Are Powerful: Our Ancestors Speak Through Us

This book is a publication of

To the youth realizing the power within themselves
to add pride to their name.
Your ancestors speak through you!

Acknowledgments

Thank you to the youth poets who contributed their powerful words to this book. Special thank you to the numerous schools that provided us the opportunity to present our poetry workshops for your students during the 2022-2023 school year. We look forward to continuing those partnerships. We greatly appreciate the Caring for Denver Foundation, Arts In Society, Bonfils-Stanton Foundation, Rose Community Foundation, and the City of Denver for providing the funding necessary to publish, celebrate, and distribute books of poetry written by underserved youth as part of our school-based programs (workshops and open mic events), all to encourage creative expression that reduces isolation, increases self-confidence, and increases the use of poetry and spoken word for coping and resilience.

Foreword

Welcome to "Our Words Are Powerful," a yearly youth-written book of poetry from the Denver area edited, published, and distributed by Words To Power. Our last 2 themes have been "The Struggle Is Real, So Is Our Resilience" and "We Are Here For A Reason." For 2023, "Our Ancestors Speak Through Us" theme inspired even more powerful words from youth in our poetry workshops and beyond. They give us a sense of hope and pride. We know you will agree.

For those who do not know about our organization: Words To Power conducts highly engaging and culturally relevant spoken word poetry workshops for Brown and other underserved youth in elementary, middle, and high schools in the Denver metro area and throughout Colorado. We partner with schools to produce poetry events with multiple participating classes coming together to share their spoken word with each other. Words To Power publishes a yearly youth-written poetry book, with most submissions coming from our workshop participants. Every summer, we host a book release event with contributors reading their poetry for their families and the greater community. Words To Power also collaboratively organizes quarterly community open mic events featuring youth who consistently participate in our programs.

The Words To Power logo draws inspiration from many sources. The overall structure is modeled after a corn plant, as our workshop curriculum uses it as a metaphor. The raised fist reminds us of our power to create change, as social justice movements before us have struggled to achieve. The scrolls on either side pull from Indigenous books in Mexico, as symbols of speech (thus the accompanying image from a codex of people talking to each other). Taken together, our words and power come from our roots.

Table of Contents

Powerful Voices by Valerie (age 8)

I am the dream
of my ancestors.
I come from God.
I will always remember the menudo
my mom makes me
with love and spiciness.
On my shoulders,
I carry the love of my family.
In the mirror,
I see the power of me!
With my voice,
I can sing and speak.
I will never forget my family.
I live in a beautiful world.
I surround myself with the power of me,
the strength of me.
I can carry the love of my family.
With our voices,
we can speak for the ones
who do not have voices.
I reach out
for the power that I
and other people need.
I have the power
that God gave me.
I keep the love
and kindness
that my family gave me.
In my eyes,
I see the power
that is coming to me.

What We Can Do in the World by Jaila Rivera (age 9)

In our hands,
we bring unity to the world
so we can be the change.
Together,
we have the power to do
the best we can.
We are the motivation
in the world.
We try our best to spread it.
With our voices,
we can speak the truth.
We are the sacrifices
of our families.
We will never forget
what we could be in this world.

The Real World by Viviana Jade Martinez (age 9)

Together,
we can show who we are.
We do not sit around
and hope.
We must work for it.
You need to show who you are.
We need to speak for our rights.
Stand up for good
and not bad.
We can create unity.
The power inside of us
can change the world.
Do not sit
and hope.
We need to work for it.
Our roots are strong.
We need to be confident.

What Life is Like by Jaycie (age 9)

When I look down,
I now see the difference.
I feel scared of what people think.
Now I don't.
I look at everyone.
I might be different
but I look the same.
I am a different color.
I am friends with people
who are not the same color as me.

I will never forget where I come from.
I promise myself.
I will always love where I come from
I am Mexican American
and proud of my people.
From our voices,
a powerful warrior comes out.
We can make a team,
so that means we are all friends,
even though we do not know each other.
We do not know
how much our hands can hold.
You know
we are stronger together.

Hands of My Parents Rise With Us by Damian D. (age 10)

I come from a world
of hope and generosity.
My parents' show
their determination
every day
for me.
Their sacrifices
inspire me
to rise to the top.
I imagine me
floating up in the sky
with angels.
I can rise
with the love
of my parents,
making me
go to college
and to be wealthy.

Un Sueño de Dios by Bella Ariel Chavez (age 10)

Yo soy un sueño de dios
y de mi familia.
Their love is like a flower.
Vengo de gente
que tiene amor por mí.
My culture is a culture like none other.
Even though I have Mexican blood,
life can still be challenging.
Dreams go through my veins.
My heart tells me to follow my dreams.
It tells me to not stop,
even if I have ups and downs.
It tells me to keep going.
En el espejo,
veo una niña bella y hermosa.

Don't Let Anyone Break You by Analia Martinez (age 10)

Don't ever let anyone
break your soul.
You have to stand
on your own.
You have two feet
to fight.
There are some people
who would not care if you fall.
So,
don't give them the satisfaction.
Hold your head up high
and put a smile on your face.

Building Something Strong by Angel Lopez (age 10)

With are voices,
we can inspire people
by grabbing success
and placing it in our hearts.
We can speak
and fight
for our country.
In our hands,
we can hold our dreams
for success.
Together,
we can bring unity
and make a strong community.

Together by Faith Ibarra (age 10)

I am mi madre's hopes.
I am the sunshine in her eyes.
In my dreams,
I wish she gets better
from sickness.
Together,
mi madre and I
cannot be separated,
nor torn apart.
When our voices join,
we make a beautiful melody.
When she looks in the mirror,
I see a person who loves me
and takes care of me.
When we join our hands,
we become powerful
together.
To mi madre,
I am her most special,
prized possession,
her whole world.

Our Dreams by Eva Hernandez (age 10)

In my dreams,
I imagine a world
I can work with,
even though
it might be hard.
Through all the paths
that we face,
we can still make it,
even if we get stuck
from the bad choices we make.
But even if it is wrong,
we still try to make it through.
Some people might do things
that are bad,
like trying to take our thoughts
into a pool
and sink them,
until our big thoughts are gone.
We must keep our thoughts heathy
and strong,
trying hard to lead us
to success.

This is my message
for the people across borders
and across the world:
Every person matters.
We are all equal
as part of humanity,
even if we only speak Spanish
or any other language.
We are not different.
We are all people
and we all matter.
I stand for my people
and others.
We are
who we are.

I Am Who I Am by Jaslyn Jade Kohmuench (age 10)

I am shy
like a fish swimming away
from a fishing rod.
When I look in the mirror,
I realize I am who I am.
In my dreams,
I imagine myself being successful
and achieving all my goals.
With our voices,
we can tell people who we actually are.
In our hands,
we hold all the courage,
telling ourselves that we believe.
Together,
we can help each other to achieve our dreams.
We are powerful together.

We Have Rights to All by Layla Casillas (age 10)

We are human.
I stay positive and respect others.
In my dreams,
we imagine having rights for all.
We all look in the mirror and we see beautiful,
handsome,
strong,
powerful,
kind,
loving,
unique,
guys,
women,
girls,
and boys.
We come from a loving,
hard-working family.

This is Me by Giovanni Dorrance (age 10)

I am the dreamer
who dreams to put smiles
on people's faces.
With my voice,
I lead us into the future.
We help
and give
to those in need.
We speak
for those who need something
without greed.

Intelligence Passed Down by Nate (age 10)

I come from my intelligent ancestors
who were ready
to sacrifice themselves
for me,
a powerful,
intelligent boy
with dreams
of helping the world.
We are a strong community
who will save the planet.

A Soldier for My Ancestors by Mazrael Chavez (age 10)

I am a soldier
fighting for the sacrifices
of my ancestors
and my family.
In my dreams,
I see a soldier
holding the world
on his shoulders.
I see someone
who can create a better future
for me
and my family.
When I close my eyes,
I see my ancestors
giving me hope
when I am down.
My enemies' pain,
jealousy,
and hate
just make me stronger.
I surround myself
with the feelings
of my ancestors.
I always feel safe
because I have God and Jesus
by my side.
I am the hero
when others are down.

Pride of Our Ancestors by Jaylynn (age 10)

In our hands,
we fight for an equal life
and community.
We always should have the power
to show our culture,
the strength
of our ancestors' roots.
Our ancestors help us,
push us.
Sometimes,
we want to change
for other people
but you should not change for others.
They might not like your culture
but that does not matter.
You need to like yourself
for who you are.
People might make fun of you,
but they just do not understand you.
Do not let some humans mess up your life.
Do not feel ashamed
of your culture.
Be proud
of who you were born
to be.

We Are Here for Each Other by Layla (age 10)

I am the light
in the dark,
showing my people hope
when they do not know
what is going to happen next.
I know my words are powerful.
I choose to believe
that we can get through hard times,
that we all can.
In my dreams,
I see my ancestors
cheering me on
to share my culture
and fight for what I think is right.
I can show my star
shining bright
because I am the hope
everyone needs.
Everyone's words
can make a difference
in the world.
Our community can come together.
When one person is in pain,
we all feel it.
We are all here
for each other.
We all suffer
when one person does.
We are all here
for each other.

Respect and Honor for Who You Are by Nelli Ochoa (age 10)

In our hands,
we carry strength,
power,
and color
of our ancestors,
who suffered
and made a good life
for each other.
We come from good,
respected people
who actually looked out
for each other.
Vengo de unas vidas
lleno de problemas
que cambian mucho
más mejor.

Our Future Will Wait by Tadeo Martinez (age 10)

I come from my mom's hopes
and dreams.
I am a fighter for my country
and nation.
On my shoulders,
I carry my pain
and happiness.
In our hands,
we hold our future
like how our ancestors did.

Dream by Zoe Casillas (age 10)

I am the love
of my parents.
I come from their souls.
When I look in the mirror,
I see a person
with many dreams
of me
accomplishing many things.
With our voices,
we can make a change
so people are really heard.
In our hands,
we can change
the way the community really is.
Together,
we can do so many things.
We are a strong community,
filled with people
who stick up for one another
and love each other.
All communities should work together
and have dreams for one another.
I am one of many
in a strong community,
a strong community who never gives up,
who never dies
and never fights.
At least,
I hope that's my dream.

Stairs of Life by Valeria Rojas (age 10)

We are all on a staircase,
taking a step
each time we age.
Sometimes,
you get tired
and feel like giving up.
Your ancestors will push you up
to get to the next steps.
Sometimes,
you might fall.
You will get up
and keep walking.
Many people
will be on the same step as you.
Others will be above.
You can watch and learn from them.
Then,
you will see those beneath you,
learning from you
taking each step to reach your dreams,
even when it gets hard.

Thank You for Everything by Axel Rodriguez (age 11)

I come from a world full of dreams.
I get inspiration from my mom.
I will always remember
how good she raised me.
I will always love her.
In my dreams,
I imagine me in the NFL.
I know I have the power to make it.
I believe in myself.
Thank you to my mom
for everything.
I love you.

La Fuerza by Ayden De Gabriel (age 11)

Yo soy un niño
que tiene la fuerza
de su raza.
Vengo de Puebla, México y
mis ancestros valientes.
En el espejo,
veo un niño
orguloso de su raza.
En mis sueños,
imagino que estoy cargando
las palabras
de mis antepasados
en mi mente,
como caballos amontonándose
antes de una tormenta.
Con nuestras voces,
podemos tener poder,
comunidad,
responsabilidad,
corazon,
y fuerza.

Fairness to the People by Bryanna Hardy (age 11)

We are all a family
who will not punish people
for being different.
We are not the prisoners
in a jail cell
who were punished.

They think they can hide all the pain
with the green armor they hide.
The liquor store is right down the block
and they think they can ban their sorrows.
But they can embrace their culture
instead of drowning in regret.

They still have a chance,
so they raise their signs
for equality.
They can still make a change in the world
and rewrite history.
They say
fairness to gay people,
black people,
indigenous people,
and all other people
who support their lives
and how they live.
Our culture is how we tell our story.
BE FREE!
BE FREE,
FOR IF YOU ARE FREE,
YOU ARE HAPPY.
LIVE
AND MAKE YOUR ANCESTORS PROUD.

Our Culture and Ancestors by Andrea Zapata Soledad (age 11)

I come from Mexico and my ancestors.
I get inspiration
from their sacrifices and struggles.
We have their memories and culture.
We have their roots.
We are strong human beings
because of the world
they created with their hands.
In the mirror,
I see myself helping my family,
working to help my mom and dad
the way they helped me.
On my shoulders,
I have hope,
I have a future
to create this world a better place.
In my dreams,
I imagine someone
who will be successful in life.
I believe that we all have hope,
and with our rights make this world
what our ancestors created for us.
In our hands,
we make this world a better place,
and fight for what's right for us.
We find strength in our hands and connect,
so we can bring unity.
In our hands,
we work together for a better life,
and for a world that's equal.
Our roots help us become better people.
We have memories from our ancestors
to be powerful.
We have our own super powers
to make this world the place
our ancestors hoped it would be.

El Mexicano by Gabriel (age 11)

Yo soy Mexicano.
Mexicanas son mi raíces,
con padres
que no son de aquí.
Soy el orgullo de ellos,
viviendo en mi
y mis hermanos.
En el espejo,
veo una persona
llena de sueños
que se van a cumplir.
Con nuestras voces,
podemos inspirar a mi gente,
a mi raza.
En nuestras manos,
nosotros podemos cambiar nuestro futuro
de nuestra gente.
Juntos,
podemos trabajar
con nuestra gente.
Somos mexicanos de raíz.
Con mi gente,
somos fuertes.

We Can Fight For Our Future By Jessie Leyva (age 11)

I am the keeper of my future,
and in my future,
my ancestors give me the strength I need
to fight racism and bullying.
I will never forget my culture,
keeping it with me forever.
We can choose
to inspire the people around us.
I hope one day
everyone stops being racist
and live a better life
by not eating junk food,
instead eating healthier.
I hope for this earth to be better,
for people to stop littering
and teach kids the same.

Poderosas by Joshua Ramirez (age 11)

We are personas poderosas
con hermosos sueños.
We accomplish our dreams
with hope
for the future
and motivation
in ourselves.
I know this
because this is the way
famous people
are where they are now.
They accomplished their dreams
with hope
and motivation.
So can we.

I Am a Dreamer by Jaimie Navarrete (age 11)

I am a dreamer!
I am powerful!
I am a helper to my family!
I come from my ancestors,
my family,
and our sacrifices.
Their struggles inspire me
to help other people
around me.
In the mirror,
I see someone powerful,
someone kind.
I surround myself
with people
who will help me
accomplish my goals
for the future.
In my dreams,
I imagine becoming a better person.
I can create something
that will help other people follow their dreams.
I imagine myself changing the world!

Words of Power for Humanity by Josue Ramos (age 12)

I am my mom's dreams.
She lifts me up
with her words
when I fall.
I come from a family
with dreams
that fly with words.
In the mirror,
I see a man
with a grateful mind.

"Freedom" Is Not Really Freedom by Adam Nehls (age 12)

The pledge of allegiance
talks about freedom
for our country.
But there is one question:
Where is the freedom?
Why do white people only get freedom?
Why do white people get to shame people
for their COLOR?
What if I was blue?
What if I was pink,
red,
orange,
or any other color?
Does it matter
if I have food stamps?
Does it matter
if someone wants to be a girl
or a boy?
Does it matter
if 2 men are holding hands?
It does not.
It does not matter
if a black man
is wearing a hoodie,
or walking,
or breathing.
It does not matter
if a Muslim woman
is wearing a hijab
and you do not like it.
It does not matter
if someone is white,
Mexican,
Hispanic,
black,
Indian,

Native American,
Muslim,
woman,
man,
or anything.
Does it matter
if a girl is showing her shoulders?
No.
Girls should not be scared to go to school
to be shamed for wearing clothes,
or being called names,
or getting sexually assaulted.
But nope,
they are.
They end up wearing clothes
that cover up their whole body
because they are scared.
"'Liberty and justice for all."
There is no justice for all.
Admit it,
there is only justice
for white men.

Let Me Live by Adam Nehls (age 12)

Every day,
I live in fear.
Every day,
I wake up in the morning
wondering,
"Why,
why,
why?"
Why do I live in fear?
I walk home in fear.
I walk home,
thinking
that I might get

sexually assaulted,
kidnapped or
just mentally abused
by a stranger.
Why do I live in fear?
I go to school every day
to be scared,
worried
that something bad will happen.
I always laugh with my friends
to get me out of the worry
that consumes me.
But when I am not talking to them,
it always comes back to me.
Why do I live in fear?
When I am away from home,
I fear
of what will happen
when I am not looking.
It happened once
when I lowered my hopes,
so,
I always keep my hopes up.
Why do I live in fear?
I am 12 year old!
I should not be scared
to walk the streets,
go to school,
or even be away
from my home and family!
But this is the world.
You have a right to be scared.
That is the world right now,
living in fear.

To The Fullest by Emilio Abeyta (age 12)

In our hands,
we are at the top of the food chain,
as big as a great dane.
We are not the same,
but most of us live in pain
like the animals we have slain.
We are killing again and again.
We are to blame
for the stuff that keeps us sane
cause most of us are plain.
But why are we here?
Is it just to fear,
hear,
and steer
our lives away?
But not today.
I do not want my future to decay,
for us to be slaves,
for us to pay
with our lives in the devil's cave.
But what is the point?
It is too late for us now.
Our fate may be given to us
by hell hounds.
Maybe it will all end with a sound,
but sooner
or later
we will come face to face
with one of our haters.
They might want to feed you
to their gator
within the walls
of their chamber.
But until we die
keep your problems
and worries aside,
keeping your prayers,
thoughts,

and ideas alive,
so you may thrive.
Do not cry,
you are not done yet.
We were all sent here
for a reason,
yes.
Now it is your turn
to go
and live your life.
It does not have to be the coolest
or smoothest,
but you should live it
to the fullest.

Justice by Ezmei (age 12)

Why?
Why us?
Why do us girls
never get justice?
Us girls
should not be scared
to wear
clothes
we are comfortable in.
I am wearing pajamas,
Hello Kitty pajamas.
Those attract you?
We are women.
I am 12,
not 30.
I am still growing.
Let me
be me.
I want to wear
crop-tops
and ripped jeans.
But I am scared
that every time
I go to the store,
someone is behind me,
looking.
It is okay for 50 year-old men
to look at 13 year-olds
like they are 30?
We need justice.
We will continue
to fight
for our community.

World by Ezmei (age 12)

I wish this world
was normal.
We have racism,
raping,
shootings,
break-ins.
We are human.
We are all
supposed to be family,
not making everyone
uncomfortable.
We need
to make this world
better.
We have the power
to fight.
We have the power
to fight for this
to stop.
Little girls are getting scared
to walk,
just across the street
to meet a friend.
They should not feel like this.
We will fight
until things are equal.

I Will Speak by Valeria Cardona (age 12)

I am a Mexican
with big dreams.
I live to be proud.
With my voice,
I speak.
I never give up.
I always have my words
and will speak.
I will speak
and shout
until I am heard.

College by Lavean (age 12)

In my dreams,
I imagine
climbing my way up.
It will be a time to discover who you are,
a path to your own success.
I believe
I will keep on trying
to get a brighter future.
I try to motivate myself
and get inspiration.
I choose
to keep working hard
and inspire others.

Believe by Karen Molina (age 12)

I come from a family
who will always be there
for me,
helping when I need them.
They try to give me
and my brothers
a better future.
They give us advice
if we do something wrong.
They give us hope.

In the mirror,
I see myself
fighting for people,
trying to stop racism,
and making the world
a better place.

I ask you to do the same.
Care for others
like you care
for your family.
Make a future
by helping your brother
or sister
to be someone
in this world.
Do not just help your family.
You can also help people
who need jobs
or a place to stay.

So, believe in yourself
so we can believe in each other.

My Story by Manny (age 13)

I am the warm filling
inside the masa.
I am sometimes spicy
but sometimes
I can be sweet.
I have a protective layer of husk.

I come from my ancestors' land.
For some people,
an alacran
might be bad luck
but for me,
it means my land.
Like an alacran,
I protect my family.

Money by Manny (age 13)

Money can be happiness
but sometimes it can cause problems.
It will change people's lives.
It can be for good
or bad.
Money can be a blessing
but sometimes it can be a curse.
It will change a homeless person's life
but will make a rich person
more greedy.
Money is tool
so use it correctly.

My Story by Gial (age 13)

My name is Gial,
eyes like a dark oak tree,
hair like a solar eclipse.

I come from the Dinka tribe
of South Sudan.
My country is a new country,
the last in Africa.

After the first Sudanese war,
Sudan was divided,
North and South.

My parents had it rough,
but had better lives
when they were young.

My mom comes from Aweil.
Her people known for their intelligence.
My mom was the smartest one in the city.

My dad comes from Juba,
the capital of South Sudan.
He started his own company.

Then the Second Sudanese War happened.
They had to flee.

My Home by Gial (age 13)

My country's flag has meaning:
Black for African Black Skin;
Red for the sweat and blood to claim our independence;
Green for agriculture, wealth, and verdant land;
White for the peace that my country has accomplished;
Blue for the Nile River;

Yellow for the future and to guide us to it.

But my people face stereotypes.
I face stereotypes.
"Don't you live in a mud house?"
"Do you have water in Africa?"
"Don't you like eating fufu and rice?"

Being a Muslim,
I also face stereotypes.

"Do you bomb planes?"
"Don't bomb my house!"
"You people should never exist."

There is a path of darkness,
when people are disrespectful.
If I retaliate,
the path of darkness gets darker
and darker.

But I think of a path of light.
Each time I am nice to people,
they are nice back.

The path of light gets brighter.

When I reach the path of light,
I can relax.

I am in a place
where I visit my grandma,
a place where I celebrate with my tribe,
a place where everyone knows me,
a place where you can go anywhere
without fearing getting lost,
a place where I am safe,
no matter what:
South Sudan,
my home.

The Colors Of Mexico by Evelyn Moreno (age 13)

I am a Mexican flag
I come from the past.
I represent culture
and stories
within an eagle
holding a snake
in my mouth.
We work hard
and do the things we love
for our culture.
We rise high up in the sky
showing pride
for who we are.
We all shine
as a shiny star in space.
We show people
who we are
letting them see
our culture.
We show our traditions.
Our traditional dances
show colorful effort
and pride.
Once Day of the Dead comes,
we do a traditional dance
to show respect
and to celebrate our
dead family members.
We are colorful
as a rainbow
with bright colors.
We flow with the beat,
dance to it
with our hearts.
These are the colors
of my culture.

Growing Butterfly by Evelyn Moreno (age 13)

I am a butterfly
that starts off
as an egg,
showing
a new life!
Once I was a baby
that feeds off of food,
as a larva would eat plants.
After I have gathered strength,
I start to grow
and learn,
holding onto information
like a chrysalis.
The information I kept
for so long,
adding onto it,
starts to become something useful
for my mindset.
I use this knowledge
for school,
to better understand.
I can then get a job
and go to college.
I am hatching
from my womb
after years or months,
as I flap my wings
to start my own journey.
With these beautiful colors,
shining with pride,
I fly away with peace.
Once I have started my journey,
I will be more responsible
and accountable,
a leader
to influence others.
This is my life
as a butterfly.

Good Enough by Jasmine Mares (age 13)

Mexican background,
but born in Colorado.

Never witnessing the beauty
of where my family
is from.

Growing up,
being the only child
with dark brown hair,
like a freshly brewed coffee,
a skin tone like hot chocolate
with extra milk.

Being asked,
why I do not have "normal skin."
Being told,
"You do not look Mexican."

Basing myself
on other people's opinions.

Not feeling tan enough.
Not feeling light enough.
Not feeling good enough.

A storm of pressure
rains upon me,
slowly fading
into a soft drizzle,
made possible
with the help
of friends
and family.

Making it easier
to turn away
from the negative.

Being myself
for myself.

Being told
I resemble my Grandmother,
my chocolate eyes glistening
like caramel in the sunlight,
providing memories of her.

Learning about my culture.
Growing into myself.
No longer changing for others.

Embracing who I am.

Game of Life by Axel (age 13)

You are in the field,
waiting
for the chance
to get the ball.
You run,
catch the ball.
Now is your time
to shine.
You may get tackled
by responsibilities
but you can get back up.
Your family
and friends watch,
waiting
for you to succeed.
Always do your best.
Do not let the pressure
make you panic.
50 yards away,
priorities set,
nobody can stop you.
Keep running,
do not stop.
The negative thoughts
slip in.
Now is not the time.
Everyone
believes in you,
do not think
about letting them down.
Think for yourself.
You are unstoppable
and you know it.
20 yards away,
too fast
to be stopped.
In your own flow,
breath,

you are almost there.
You see an opponent
fixated on taking you down
with insecurity
and expectations.
But you are not alone.
Beside you
are your teammates,
there to protect you,
help you.
10 yards away
until you reach your dreams,
keep going
no point in stopping.
Nobody is holding you back anymore.
Touchdown!
You did it,
achieve your dreams,
telling those haters
to back off.
But,
you know
this is far from over.
Keep running
and do not stop.

Tree of Knowledge by Axel (age 13)

I lift my people
with charisma and bravery.
I am the root of my ancestors.
We keep growing,
learning from our elder trees,
sprouting into our prime.
I lift others,
planting the seed
of success
and feeding it the water
of responsibilities.

We may have fallen before,
during five centuries of oppression,
but that is the past.

Branches may fall,
yet we still stand,
brown,
beautiful,
and stronger
after everything we face.
Biligana tries to poison us
with tree killer.
Little did they know
we grew stronger.
Chainsaws of oppression
try to cut me down.

I am not alone.
Beside me
are my ancestors,
toughest of them all.
They give me the strength
to carry my burdens.
I stand strong
like an oak tree.

My People by Candy (age 14)

For my people
who are selfless,
who are caring.
Would they be disappointed
of how white people
shaped their land,
silencing and looking down
on our people?
Would they help us
with how today's society
teaches us selfish things?
Can they help us?

I Am the Pencil by Candy (age 14)

I am the pencil but different.
I am small.
I am dull.
But I am not breakable.
I keep trying.
I am a yellow pencil.
Yellow is kind.
Yellow is peaceful.
The paper is my life,
my existence.
I sketch my world and life.
Sometimes
an eraser is useful
for the mistakes I make.
After the sketch,
I do line art,
so I can make my life
more clear and smooth.
After the line art,
I add color for my life
to be more creative and lively.

The Fight by Alexis (age 14)

I am
the person
who will
represent our culture
con corazon
y sangre,
as I fight
for
my people.
I come from
the struggle
of my ancestors.
They speak life
into me.
When I look in the mirror,
I see
someone powerful,
someone ready
to take on the world.
By fighting
through my emotions,
yo soy fuerte
y poderoso.
In my dreams,
I imagine the future
with freedom
for my culture.

Taking It Slow by Antonio Helper (age 14)

Our ancestors speak through us
only if you want to hear.
Some with eyes of red
and burning smoke
that get lips
into feeling the float
causing the crack
in the creator's throat.
They hold these crutches within
to expel the sorrow
or the pain.
This is the ancestors' pain,
the float,
only if we do not choose the path
of doing dope.
But this is only possible
if you listen
and walk the Red Road
to the purified side
of the soul.
This is the way
we can listen to our ancestors
and relatives
through just taking it slow.

Nightmares and Dreams by Daniel Zuniga (age 14)

I am just a Mexican kid
living in America,
the land
that is supposed to be just
and free.
But every day
I go outside,
I see a place
out to get my family.
In 2016,
I had nightmares
of a racist white man
getting elected as president
and removing the people of my culture,
as residents of this country,
while calling us murderers,
drug dealers,
and stealers.
That nightmare had come true,
and every day
I feared the men
preaching the red,
white,
and blue.
People I used to see as nice
now threatening to call ICE.
Even now,
I visited Texas,
the land
that used to be owned
by my ancestors,
and to my shock,
it was full of white patriots
screaming racial slurs
about my culture.
At one point,
I thought
that things would never change,

that my Mexican heritage
would keep me trapped in a cage.
When I remember my ancestors
fighting for our freedom,
I want to fight back
for them.
So,
I will take a page
from their book,
and fight for a land
that is truly free,
one that allows me
to be me.
We are workers,
we are fighters,
we are the backbone
of this nation.
Once we realize that,
then we will take this country
and change it,
for our ancestors,
for ourselves,
and for the future generations.
We will make a land
that is truly free
for all,
and grab the key
to the cage
we were locked in,
embracing our culture
and being able
to finally
win.

Life is Like by Elina Pasillas (age 14)

Life is just like a drawing.
There has to be a sketch
in your head
for what you want in life.
You try to erase mistakes you make
but they never fully go away.
No matter how hard you try,
no matter what you do,
someone will hate.
But there is no need to change
for someone,
as long as you are satisfied.
Sometimes you use different techniques
to get better.
When the pencil breaks,
it is like losing part of yourself,
so keep sharpening
until you are happy.

More Than An Appearance by Ema Villapando (age 14)

My body developed
sooner than others.
Men staring at my chest,
not feeling safe.
Men grabbing my chest.

Was it my fault?

The guilt I carry
feels like going up Mount Everest
with a boulder on my shoulder.

Sweater upon sweater,

every inch of my body
covered up to feel safe.

Men are like bears
and I am a jar of honey.
They cannot stop grabbing,
always so provoked.

Male validation
seems like a compliment.
I like compliments.
But then it gets so bad.
You start wearing revealing clothes
just for the admiration.
All the stares I get
make my heart sink
deeper and deeper.

The question,
"Why me?"
always going through my head.

But I still tell myself
It was not my fault.
I am not an object.
I have worth.
I have self-respect.

I do not need validation.
I am more than my appearance.
I am a good friend,
a good daughter,
a smart student,
a person.

We Are All the Same by Efrain Huerta (age 14)

In our eyes Latinos,
and Latinas
are hard workers,
trying to make money
and a life in America.
But to others,
all they see
is illegal Mexicans
stealing jobs,
and drug cartels.
But if only they put
the stereotypes aside,
they would see
that we put sweat and tears,
making our hands rough
to make money
and start a nice
and normal life
to live in America.
They would see
that we are always willing to give a hand.
But some day,
when the stereotypes end,
they will see
that we are all the same
no matter
what race
you are.

Mi Gente by Esperanza (age 14)

Para mi gente morena
que vienen de la bandera
verde, blanco, y rojo,
con sangre Azteca,
Chicano/a,
o simplemente Mexicano,
que siempre tendrán la cabeza en alto.
Trabajan de día
y de noche,
haciendo todo
para mantener a su familia.
Celebran a su reina
y rey
de vestido verde
y de oro cada diciembre.
Para mi gente
que cruza la frontera
para poder mantener a su familia,
hasta a veces tener que mirar por atrás,
no más para quedarse en los Estados Unidos
y no ser llevados.
Tiene que vivir
con ser llamados narcos,
borrachos,
y criminales,
por todo lo que dice el publico.
Les dicen que venden drogas,
hacen cocaína
y son narcotraficantes
que matan a los que los hacen enojar.
Teniendo que escuchar
que se vayan de donde vinieron,
cuando todo lo que quieren hacer
es mantener a su familia.
Para mi gente
que tiene que ser separado de su familia,
que se preocupan
que algun dia

no van a poder ver
a su familia
y tener que crecer sin sus papas.
Los niños tienen
que ver sus papas llevados
por la migra,
esperarando años
para verlos
y estar con ellos.
Teniendo qué ver la migra entrar a tu casa
para llevar a tu familia,
cuando todo lo que quieren hacer
es soportar a su familia.
Para mi gente
de piel morena
que celebran su bandera
de los colores verde,
blanco,
y rojo,
con música bonita
y orgullosa.
Cuando uno baila,
todo lo que hacen es sonreir.
Su comida está hecha por la calle
con una lonchera
que siempre será mejor
que la comida falsa llamada "Mexicana".
Sus fiestas celebran a su madre,
vestida de esos tres colores
que representamos con nuestras vidas.
Para los mexicanos
de todo color
que siempre tendrán la sangre mexicana en su venas
y siempre tendrán la cabeza en alto.
No dejarán de luchar
por lo que se merecen.

Teary Brown Eyes by Ethan (age 14)

The sun is gone.
I stay,
the sky dark
like the ocean,
stars shining,
wind moving.
The pain slowly goes away,
as one tear
falls on the grass.

Opportunities by Yassine (age 14)

I am a grinder,
working hard,
non-stop
toward opportunities,
like time never stops ticking.
I come from an average family
that did not have much.
We are doing well now,
able to experience opportunities
that our parents never had.
When I look in the mirror,
I see a warrior
fighting for my true passion.
In my dreams,
I imagine myself
accomplishing my dreams
of becoming a pilot,
all to allow my parents
to never have to live the life
they had in their past,
a new beginning for all of us.

The Reality by Mai Van (age 14)

For my loved ones
living in the luscious rainforest
full of trash,
selling lottery tickets,
begging,
pleading,
hoping to make an earning;
with houses filled with mistakes
and regret from the past,
surrounded by smelly,
unsanitary markets,
and the uncertainty of living a happy life.
This is our cruel reality.
For my loved ones
being made fun of
because of our eyes,
accents,
language;
embarrassed of our food,
culture,
parents,
and who we are;
harassed on the streets
with no help,
no luck,
and certainly no future.
This is our cruel reality.
For my loved ones
being romanticized,
targeted,
sexualized
because of our eyes,
clothes,
and "innocent" looks;
trying to mimic us,
become us,
be us.
This is our cruel reality.

For my loved ones
who are able to overcome this,
who are able to dance happily
with their straw hats,
flowing Áo dài,
quạt tay;
those able to happily eat our bánh bo,
bánh pía,
bánh kếp
without a care in the world.
This is our happy reality.
Let us rise
and take a hold
of our culture,
our identity,
and ourselves.
We are the ones
who get to judge
who we are,
what we do,
and what we wear.
Let us not romanticize others.
Let us not judge others.
Let us celebrate
and rise together
as a whole.
This is the happy reality.

Sensitive by Roberto Ochoa (age 14)

My name is Roberto,
eyes brown
like Goomba's feet,
4 foot 11,
around the same height
as Danny Devito.

Sensitive.
I wish I was less sensitive.
My dad always wants me
to be a man.

If I get my feelings hurt
and I start to cry,
my eyes swell up,
turn red,
and fill with tears.
He tells me,
"Stop crying.
You are not a girl."

If I ask my dad
to do something for me,
he says
"Do it yourself,"
when he knows I cannot.

He says,
"When I want something done,
I do it myself."
or
"Me and your mom
will not always be there.
You need to learn."

But I am still a kid.
I want to be more hardworking,
but I take the easy way out.

In school,
I rush,
I do the bare minimum.
I talk myself out of doing things
that require a lot of work.

When my dad looks at me,
I want him
to say to himself,
"WOW,
he really has grown up
to be a man.
Now he can do things
without help from his dad."

I need to show him
that I am hardworking.

I know I can be a man
because of what my dad
pushes me
to do.

I know
I can be a man
who makes my dad proud.

God's Dreams by Aguilera (age 14)

I am a kid with the biggest dreams.
I will always remember
the blood,
sweat,
and tears
that I put into my life.
I come from a family with big dreams
The struggles make me work more hard
In the mirror,
I see what God has the power to create.
I surround myself with God's people.
I reach out to God to get to my goals.

Ode to a Cell Phone by Alijah Walker (age 15)

Hours of screen time,
multiple texts,
if this isn't a drug,
what's next?
Thousands of videos,
millions of teens,
hundreds of kids
are now trapped in screens.
The satisfying tap
of the glass screen,
millions of stories
can be seen.
The peel of the factory plastic
warms my heart.
Good luck taking a phone
and a teen apart.

Who Am I If I Can't Be Me? by Amelia (age 15)

I am a person
with hope and dreams,
a person who has goals
that are yet to be achieved.
I hold the strength
of my ancestors
to motivate me
for the future I seek.
I come from a family
who do not think
before they speak.
I bleed from the wounds
they inflicted on me.
But I still stand tall,
knowing that I will never fall.
In the mirror,
I see the girl
I am afraid to meet,
the girl
who was so afraid
to speak.
This girl,
who I used to be,
is now standing
right in front of me,
reminding me of the past
that I never want to see.
In my dreams,
I imagine breaking a cycle
that is preventing me
from becoming
who I am meant to be.
These chains are holding me back
from being free.
I take the strength of my spirit
to release these chains
and turn them into wings.

Bomboclat by Amaranta Caraveo (age 15)

I put my headphones on
and boom,
boom,
I feel the bass in my veins.
All of a sudden,
I am in a magical place in my mind,
where my thoughts are put into words.
Those words taste like pop rock candy
and others taste like caramel.
My playlist is like Colorado,
bipolar:
one second,
I could be dancing
and the other,
I could be crying my heart out.
No matter the song,
I enjoy it.
There are times
when I am not listening to music
but I am still able to hear it in my head.
I hear the lyrics,
repeating like a broken record.
I feel the beat,
pounding like a loving heart
when hugging someone.

Light in the Dark by Ana (age 15)

I am the light in the darkness.
With my words,
I bring brightness.
I come from an unchangeable place,
a place where change needs to happen
but will not.
In the mirror,
I see a girl working to make herself and others better.
I have the power to change the unchangeable.
In my dreams,
I imagine peace in a world,
where everyone is equal,
with people who treat the Earth right.

Nothing Impossible by Ana (age 15)

With our voices,
we can inspire ourselves and others
to reach our future.
We can find strength together,
We have more power together.
In our hands,
we have the power
to make the impossible possible.
Our motivation will not just be life-changing.
It is world-changing.
Together,
we can use the power inside of us
to change in this world.
Together,
we can inspire the world.
We are stronger together
than apart.
We speak for the unspoken.
We speak to inspire the change
that is possible.

If I Wasn't an Indian by Andrew Romero (age 15)

Don't ask if I live in shame.
I see you looking weird,
but the image stays the same.
I don't need acknowledgment,
you don't need to know my name.
I'm different,
a savage
that's the name
that I contained.
Don't wear it out.
Don't scream with all the doubt.
I'm not suffering in vain,
like you did my ancestors,
when you scrubbed their skin with soap.
We will never stay sobbing,
growing vivid,
trying to sprout.
We make it out of the bottom,
like a seed devoured in the dirt.
I have a message that I hold
can't break me down.
I won't be hurt.
See,
my family is growing
and my ancestors aren't in pain.
If they suffered in the past,
they'll see the gift,
I grow my name:
fierce,
violent,
and cannot be controlled.
That's the name
that you gave me,
I cannot uphold.
Of course,
I won't let you conquer my city,
take my family,
and steal my crops.

If we're firmly planted,
we won't be stopped.
So,
if you plant pride
in my mind,
give me water
and light.
I'll grow.
I'll prosper,
won't be left behind.
Matter of fact,
I'll be right in front.
"I don't want to be an Indian."
"Then you're a native no more,"
ashamed of the warrior,
scared of the fight.
Shame and darkness
can't contain the light.
Living is a battle,
can't tell me that I'm wrong.
So,
why do you worry about the judgement?
It keeps misleading on.
You're a flower in the weeds,
you need to know that.
If you have pride
and dignity,
you need to show that.
We live in a way we can't control.
We're blinded
and shamed
to not claim
what we're told.
But there's rocks in the sand
that must stay grounded.
If you noticed,
that I'm one of them
then you'll see there's no challenge.
With my family that grows
and it keeps getting bigger,

like the water on the shore
when interrupted,
it ripples.
See,
I'm different.
It's a vivid spectrum.
I'm a Native in blood.
I'm not savage
or hectic
with a sign on my head.
I've painted a picture.
You see that I'm different.
I'm not an alcoholic
who drinks liquor.
I'm not a red skin
with a wild figure.
I'm not what you've hung
over my head.
If I wasn't an Indian,
I'd rather be dead.

The Garden of Flowers by Bellarae Maestas (age 15)

I am a warrior,
a leader.
I am a resilient flower,
a flower
that comes from strong roots.
With these strong roots,
I can grow
into my higher self.
I come from a garden of flowers,
flowers
that lead me to be me.
These flowers
are strong and courageous.
They are my light
in the darkness.
When I look in the mirror,
I see my ancestors,
the ancestors
who fought their hardest
for their land,
the ancestors
who never lost hope or faith.
I see my ancestors
who did everything to protect
THEIR land and families.
In my dreams,
I imagine
what life was like
before I was planted in soil.
I imagine
what the other flowers
had to go through
in order for me
to be here.
I imagine
the flowers
growing to be strong
and courageous.

Not Enough Recognition by Bellarae Maestas (age 15)

The warriors,
the warriors
who stood
where I stand today,
the warriors
who fought to live
were once
brought
to their end.
They stood where I stand.
Their once livable life
turned to dust,
nothing.
The dust collects
as their history
is not told
in the correct font.
The font is horrendous,
as it speaks of lies,
lies that were once nothing,
lies that spoke of evil,
alcoholism,
lies that lead
to more dust.
As the dust collects,
the history
is too blurry
to be seen
with the naked eye,
the history
that told the truth,
the truth
that was once
valued,
the truth
that will not be seen.

La Morena by Camila Castro (age 15)

Yo soy Mexicana,
la más oscura
compared to others,
the one
who can never catch a break
from this gloomy weather.
I beg to be freed
from the wrath of the over privileged kids
who will never understand
where I come from.
They do not want us
but want to look like us.
Our presence drives them nuts.
They would rather put us in cuffs.

Vengo de la sangre de mi madre,
de sus sacrificios y sueños
Vengo de mi herencia.
I come from the pain of my parents,
bringing gorgeous inheritance.
My blood and your blood
are the same.
So,
why do I have shame
and you have fame?

In the mirror,
I see a person who fights battles,
overcomes challenges and struggles,
a person who wants to be the pride of the family.
One day,
I will
but for today,
I stay still.
I am stuck in my pain
and I need to escape.
I have climbed over mountains,
now there is only one left.

Then I will be free.

En mis sueños,
imagino una vida mejor,
a life where I do not fear
leaving my house.
I do not fear the police
who are supposed to protect us.
I do not fear my family
leaving alive
but coming back derived from life.

Esos Ojos Cafes by Camila Castro (age 15)

In our eyes,
we see our struggles,
our pain,
our light.
They hold our past,
present,
and future.
My eyes are the same
as my ancestors held,
a shade of dark brown
that looks pitch black
until the sun shines on us
and all the intricate designs are seen.
The beauty of our eyes
are seen only then,
only seen by those who deserve it,
not by those who see me as anything but Mexican,
not by those who call me black.
Why should they see my beauty
if they cannot see me
for who I truly am
and see my culture?

My culture can never be taken away.
They can take me away
from my people and my home.
But they will still see a Mexican,
an alien.
In my eyes,
I see a girl who will live her truth
become who she wants to be,
embracing her scars
that show her past.
In my eyes,
I see a girl who will allow herself
to be happy,
forgive those who have wronged her
and treated her in a way
she did not deserve.
In my eyes,
I see a girl with beautiful tan skin,
brown eyes,
and brown hair,
a girl who can accept herself
for who she is.

Paper by Zamir (age 15)

Clear,
yet full of potential,
emotions and ideas
shown within
paper.
The smell of lead on you,
the taste of nothing
but an acidic flavor.
Like a canvas to a painter,
filled with thoughts,
rough yet smooth
filled with art.
Blank like a board,
yet able to express everything,
at one time.

Escape Getaway by Liliana Morales (age 15)

Life is like an ocean.
The waves explain life,
the moments you need to pull back.
The smell of the breeze,
quiet with no worries
no phone next to you.
Your eyes can wander,
so much more to see,
exploring more than you know.
The ocean kisses the sky
with nothing but peace of mind.
It is like a breeze,
going back and forth.
My love for a vacation
is as deep as the ocean.
The beach is a wonderland.

All for One and One for All by Colin Nguyen (age 15)

I am someone
who wants to strive
to be better
than I am now,
someone people can rely on
and say,
"wow!"
I am the dream of my parents.
I love how they prepared us,
spared us from all the troubles.
I come from generations of Asian culture,
trying to capture every moment of it,
trying to pass on prayers
to the next generation.
I want the next generation
to know the information,
so they could start conversations.
I want to be an inspiration,
so people don't get too frustrated.
In the mirror,
I see someone,
someone who has the potential to become successful,
someone who doesn't want to be regretful,
someone who avoids situations that are stressful,
someone who can overcome the struggles.
I want to be the person
I see in the mirror,
who hustles.
In my dreams,
I imagine being the best that I can be,
someone who can flow
like water in the sea.
I imagine being someone people can believe in.
I imagine it in my dreams,
but one day I will make it into a reality.

One Must Concede by Junior Reyes (age 15)

The bell rings out, the fighters clash,
their gloves meet with a thunderous crash.
A dance of footwork, a symphony of blows,
each fighter aims for his opponent´s nose.

The crowd roars with every punch,
their excitement building with each crunch.
The fighters grit their teeth and fight,
their determination shining bright.

The bell rings again, the fighters retreat,
their corners tending to each bruise and beat.
But soon they're back, ready to brawl,
for in the ring, there is no time to stall.

The fight goes on, the rounds tick by,
each fighter giving it his all to try
to come out on top, to be the best,
to leave the ring with pride in his chest.

And when the final bell does sound,
the fighters stand, their feet on the ground.
One is the victor, one must concede,
but both have proven they have what it takes to succeed.

The Weight We Carry by Ericka Itzel (age 15)

With our voices,
we can find strength within our hearts
to inspire every one of those kids
who lived like I lived growing up.
In our hands,
we hold our future.
We have the power
to choose what path to take,
to succeed or to give in
in a cell.
They said,
"Do not let your dreams rot in jail."

Together,
we can fix and lift
the wrong in the world.
Con nuestras voces,
we bring peace and unity
even when feeling
like we have no control.

We are the dreams
that our parents fought so hard
to take care of.
We speak for their culture
running through our veins,
and I pray
that my dreams do not crash
on the way.
Mami,
you will be proud.
I know that the struggle we went through
and the failed relationships
you did not mean to involve us in
will give me motivation
to keep your love in my eyes
and your strength in my heart,
as I lift the disappointment off my shoulders.

The Power of Our Ancestors by Johnathan (age 15)

Our ancestors have set the stones
for the foundation
we are building upon.
The blueprint has been set.
We are building it
to make a guideline
for generations to come.
Our ancestors have created the sparks
that made the fire
that we continue to fuel.
We are the light
that our ancestors have made
to show the path
that we continue to take.
Our ancestors are the raindrops
that made the oceans.
We are the water
that continues to fill them.
Our ancestors have started building
the world up from nothing.
They have left the world better
for generations to come.
They are counting on us
to continue building
and fix it.
We are doing what our ancestors have done:
we are making the world better
for generations to come.

Building the World by Johnathan (age 15)

With our voices,
we can be
what our ancestors
wanted to be.
We are the roots
of the seed
that they planted.
We are on the path
that they have set.
We are the sparks
that light the fire.
We are light
in the darkness.
We the roots
of this planet.
When we cut life,
we are cutting ourselves.
When we build upon this planet,
we are bettering ourselves.
We all share the same home.
We are the same.
We create,
build,
and destroy.
We are the light
to the darkness.
We are the path
to the future.
We,
as humans,
hold the future of life
in our hands.
When we make bad decisions,
it will show on the next generation of humans.

Ode to Tobi by Andy (age 16)

He is the dog version
of me and my brother.
His arrogance and laziness
is just like my brother's,
and his homeless look
and active personality
just like me.
He is ugly and expired-looking,
but always seems to win me over
with his huge eyes.
I come home after a long,
bad day
and there he is,
barking,
growling,
trying to protect our house from a threat.
I open the door
and his huge eyes meet mine.
His tail starts to waggle all over the place
as he fills up with joy.
That long,
bad day suddenly turns.

Rocky Ford by Amiya Holguin (age 16)

Hands so sweet to the heart
yet so dry with touch.
Oh how I miss you dearly.

County Road FF
goes right down memory lane.
Dirt roads and yucca plants,
oh how I miss it.

Watermelon seed spitting,
dirty boots kicking,
pumpkin patch picking,
tail gates swinging.

The remodeled train cart
turns to the "Tick Tock Shop,"
Tick Tick Ticking away
for more mysteries to be encountered.

Listening carefully
to the coyotes howling
and the 10-foot-tall bonfire crackling.

Watching you jump,
LEAP over those flames
scared me.
Oh, but how brave you were.

Your colored flannels
matched perfectly with your personality,
just as well as your pearl snaps
glowed with your gentle eyes.

Waking up to scriptures being read out loud
"He restores my soul."
"He leads me in paths of righteousness."
Psalms 23: 2-3

Your voice sang so beautifully,
as you worshiped the Lord.
Your smile was contagious,
and you lit up every room as you walked through.

With your cigarettes in your side pockets
and your Tic Tacs in the other
you had a significant smell,
a comforting smell.

Once I heard you were gone,
life did not feel…
real.
But knowing I will see you again
gives me relief.
It takes the pressure off my heart.
Oh, how I miss you.

Flower of Success by Becca W. (age 16)

We change our family's eyes,
switching them out for new ones,
inspiring them to see the positive opinions
of our choices and responsibilities.
With such little control,
let them help us reach for success,
as high as the stars.

With our hands,
we alter minds to positive outcomes,
drowning out negativity
with encouraging words
of love,
connection,
and strength,
while putting sweet aromas
into our auras.

We will raise ourselves higher,
looking back at where we came from,
a dark pit
of good and bad memories,
like a rainbow of shades.
The people we care about
are there with us,
celebrating with hugs and big smiles.

We are the future,
the role models,
children from the dirt ground
who have grown leaves and petals.
In a society suffering through death,
life,
viruses,
gun abuse,
and racism,
we build a statue
to honor those who had their stems cut short.

An Ode to Pencils by Gabriel Jaramillo (age 16)

My Pencil:
the most creative of most utensils;
able to make a reality
with ideas
as intuitive
and taken for granted
as most principles;
able to delete any of your
most dreadful mistakes;
able to accomplish great joy and happiness
or drown you in sorrow and misery;
able to warm your hearts and souls
or freeze them
in the depths of malice and despair;
always able to maintain
the creativity of the owner
like actions or gossip
in the spread of truths and love
or lies and hate.

Ode to Art by Crishawn Curry (age 16)

As lead
and the products of a tree
touch,
the piece being made
touches the heart,
creating what is known as Art.
Many people say "Art" is:
a skill to impress,
a born talent,
a pathway to wealth.
Art may be those things.
I agree one hundred percent.
Art is all of the things
people say it is.

Yet,
as humans,
we tend to overlook
the true goal
of a painting,
drawing,
building.
People cannot see
that art is the world.
Every building we walk by
once was a drawing on a blue script.
The world is made
of many settings and biomes,
creating the best inspiration
for artists'
and audiences'
field of vision.
Many colors to use,
like rainbows had babies.
Art is an explosion,
a form of telling a story,
no words needed.
Art tells a message
mere words
cannot hope to achieve.
Without art,
words would not even exist.
Art brings people together
through empathy,
joy,
and love.
Art is the world.
Art is my world.

Money by Khris Rivers (age 16)

Money,
oh money,
you rule the world,
a powerful force
that can make us swirl.
You can bring us happiness
or cause us pain,
and yet we still seek you,
again and again.
Money can buy us the finest things,
but can also be a curse.
When you have it,
it makes you outburst
in a way that changes you
for the worse.
Money,
you make us greedy
but we still chase you
like a lost puppy anyway
Money can destroy us
or build us up,
so be wise.

Ode to My Sister by Jennifer G. (age 16)

She is my only sister
and is older than me,
though I am taller than her.

She looks out for me,
makes me feel important,
and has always been there for me.

She never leaves the house
without her floral scent.
When coming home,
she makes it known by her loud voice

My sister is the same
as my mom,
always talking loudly.
as if they are screaming.

She protects the people around her
like a mother duck who protects her
little ducks when crossing the street.

I am grateful to my sister
for making me laugh,
trying to sing while washing the dishes,
and for not leaving me alone during hard times.

Thank you sister.

Listen by Meadow Yellow Hawk (age 16)

Listen
and listen carefully
while our ancestors
stand behind us
knowing
we will continue their legacy.
Listen
and listen carefully
as we say our prayers
for our ancestors
who fought
to keep our traditions alive.
We will now be able
to achieve everything
that we were deprived.
Listen
and listen carefully
for we celebrate
those who helped shape our identity,
not just ethnically,
not just inherently
but spiritually.
Just listen...

Ode to Ma by Maana Abdulkadir (age 16)

My mother
is the one
who I must obey,
sweet like the cookies
she always bakes.
She is one
who used to hold me,
clean me,
and cloth me.
No other,
my mother.
When I was to fall,
she was the one
to pick me up.
Before I could talk,
she was the one
to hear me.
Before I could walk,
she was the one
to hold me.
No one
but my mother.
She is the one
who is always there,
to listen,
to love,
and to beam.
She is the one
who wiped my tears,
knows my fears,
the one who really cares.
No other,
my mother.

Ode to Boxing by Josiah (age 16)

Dear Boxing,

From the moment
I wrapped my fists and gloved my hands,
I knew I would love you forever.
I knew you would be my forever therapist.

With restless nights of shadow boxing,
I think of moves like a chess match,
moving my feet as if I was dancing
without music.

I think of people watching me
and cheering
as I beat the air to a pulp,
listening to the 30 second
wood boards bang together.

20 seconds left,
my arms are tired,
5 seconds more,
left, right, left, jab, cross.
Ding, ding, ding.
As the noise goes off,
I look at the air
with no damage done to it.

As the crowd goes wild,
I hear by unanimous decision... THE AIRRRRR.
I drop to my knees and beat myself up.
The lesson:
you can never win
if you fight yourself.

DING, DING, DING

Your forever client,
Client #1

Ode to the Father who Taught Me the Game of Chess by Jeremiah Martinez (age 16)

When you move,
there is so much grace.
I can smell the food you made
before we played.

Win, lose, learn, think!

You taught me strategy.
You showed me the game,
to slow down to think.
You are my biggest opponent
but also my mentor.
When I look at the piece
and think about you,
I understand the goal of the game.
You are the only piece
to me
that matters.

I want it bad,
just to win,
to pin your pieces,
to trap you,
to fork you,
to dominate the board.

It is more than a game.
It is more than everything,
bonding with you.
I practice,
trying my hardest.
You say I duck.
I am just learning.
When we play,
I understand who you really are:
chess with my hero.

Love Tears by Thais Alvarez Aragon (age 16)

Dear Sunshine,

I dropped a tear
into the ocean
last night,
and I
will not stop loving you
until I find it.
Every time your eyes cry
like the sea,
I will be the sand,
that waits for you
on the shore
to dry you.

Ode to Blanco by Nataly Salas (age 16)

Playful,
running side to side
with toys.
Playing with our shoes,
trying to trip us.
Seeing how much you love to sleep
especially in the sun.
Seeing how much you love getting pet,
especially after your exhausting adventures
through the house.
Seeing you force yourself through doors
like a snake
to get to me.

Oh, how much you love me Blanco.

The Sun by Reesa Salazar-Franco (age 16)

The sun is like a Madre.
It gives me kisses every time I turn,
holds me tight and now I yearn.
It keeps me in touch with my ancestors,
allowing me to never forget the answers.
They are the only ones I will ever need,
between the sun and this ghostly seed,
the one that grows and grows.
It never slows.
Deep down,
it always knows
how my heart it races,
when I see those faces
of gueritos who could not care.
But they always seem to stare.
The sun is always there,
making sure my skin is never fair.
It is up in front so that they know
that we,
the Mexica,
will never go.
We must stay
so that they can see
that we are here
and not extinct.
We feel the string
that keeps us linked.
From the north to the south,
we are all Familia,
and that is not just word of mouth.
The sun is like a mother.
It will always keep us together.
For we,
the people of Anahuac,
will always be one
and that cannot be undone,
when we are all children
of the sun.

Malaya by Mijah Bolden (age 16)

She was as beautiful as a Friesian horse;
and as unique as a white-toothed cowry on a stranded beach shore.

She had beautiful eyes, her olive, green eyes;
They remind you of green hydrangeas.

Her hair was short and curly;
and bounced like springs.

Her complexion reminds you of brazil nuts, honey brown;
Her freckles were faint but scattered like the stars in the sky.

Her smile was bright and radiant;
like the moonlight in a dark night.

Her voice was welcoming;
just like shaking someone's hand.

Her laugh was very delightful;
and as contagious as a yawn.

Her hugs were very pleasant and warming;
just like coffee in an early morning.

Her personality was like a wild fire;
wild, free, and beautiful.

She was brave and fearless like a lion;
and as ambitious as a black mamba.

She was as strong as a diamond;
and loyal like a dog.

She was protective over the people she loved;
like a mama bear to her cubs.

If she was a color, she would be violet-blue;

ambitious, creative, independent, dignified, devoted, free, confident, loyal, and inspiring.

She is still as beautiful and amazing, just not in the flesh;
Nevertheless, she is now home in the white kingdom.

She now has her wings;
just like a butterfly out of the cocoon.

Even though my heart hankers for her;
and I'm longing for home.

She will always be here, even if I don't see her;
She is now my guardian angel and now goes everywhere I go.

If I had a chance, I would do whatever it takes to be together;
and enjoy these amazing traits again whenever.

Love you Malaya and I will miss you forever;
Like they say, "This isn't goodbye, just see you later."

Chicano Love, Chicano Power by Veneno Quezada Montoya (age 16)

I want you to say:
Chicano Power,
Chicana Power!
Now,
what does that mean?
That means
when the next pig or the next colonizer
tries to put down your brown,
the blood of the Mexica
that runs through you is a reminder
that you are not a minority,
but a revolutionary.
That means
Aztlan is not a homeland far away
but right where you stand.
So,
when you stand,
keep your chin up!
Let the spirit of the five suns
feed the Chicano fire in your soul.
That fire is sacred,
surrounding your fist,
as you wave it in the air
screaming and crying
the tears of the ancestors.
The gift from our ancestors
is the spirit of the warrior.
And the spirit of the warrior will not rest,
until we take that first breath of liberation.
But before the revolution comes,
we need to remember:
Chicano education is Chicano revolution.
Chicano revolution is Chicano liberation.
And Chicano love is Chicano power.

Ode to Football by Preston Hebert (age 17)

The football field is a battlefield,
where warriors fight with strength to score
and victory is the prize we adore.
The quarter back is a general, the leader of his troops.
He directs the offense with his voice and his moves.
The running back is a battering ram, a force of nature.
He charges through the defense like a raging creature.

The offensive line is a wall of steel, a fortress so strong.
They protect the QB like a mother's song.
The defensive line is a pack of wolves, a fierce brigade
They hunt down the ball carrier like a predator's raid.

The linebackers are like cannons, powerful and loud.
They hit the ball carrier like a thundercloud.
The defensive backs are like eagles soaring high.
They intercept the ball like a bird in the sky.
The game is a symphony, a work of art,
where every player plays their part.
The fans are the audience to the music they hear
and the players are the performers, the artists they cheer.

But win or lose, the game is the same,
a passion that burns like a never-ending flame.

Power by Christopher (age 17)

In the mirror,
I see my ancestors,
their sacrifices
on my shoulders,
the strength
of a survivor.
I surround myself
with inspiration
and motivation.
I have the power
to create my future
even though the struggle
makes me always remember
I am a survivor.
With our voices,
we can reach out to our community,
we can end cruelty.
The dreams give us inspiration
to show the power inside us
so we can bring peace
and unity.

Determination by Sgarcia (age 18)

I am a struggle
wrapped in a gift.
The key to success
knocks at my door
like time is endless.
I come from empty pockets
full of dreams.
I hear lots of screams
because I come from rocks
that but heads
until they are dead.
I am looking in the mirror,
crying on the inside,
but strength is coming out.
I am still looking in the mirror.
But this time,
I fight.
Why wouldn't I?
With determination,
despite the discrimination,
we make our way to the top.
We ignore the negativity
and never stop.
It started with our hands.
Then,
we made plans
to work hard for what we want.
We make it to the top
despite the voices and the choices
we have made.
We want success till this day.
We are
what we want to be.
So we forget what they say.
Because through blood,
sweat,
and tears,
we found the way.

An Unforeseen Future by Maqsud Hashi (age 18)

I dream about you.
I long to meet you.
You captivate my every thought.
It has been so long,
I feel like I am suffocating
on your newly found beauty,
Each layer of you
is a gift from the heavens above,
forever grateful.

Oh, I miss you!

I am ashamed
to say
that I have not learned
our love language:
poetry.
It is the backbone
of our identity.
I have yet to listen
to the sweet melody
of you.
I am not a stranger,
but I feel like one.
If you have Somali blood,
this situation is hard to grasp.

I love you.

Hoyo tells me a lot about you.
Each of her memories
burned into my brain
like a tattoo
forever
so beautiful
I am sad to say
I do not share
my mother's memories.

I wish!
As I lay here
gazing at your beauty,
I wonder how stupid
I must have been
to feel ashamed of us.

Allahu Akbar!!
Allahu Akbar!
la hawla wala quwwata illa billah!
Inna lillahi wa inna ilayhi raji'un
The smell of death
hits the nation
like a deadly virus,
knocking down the doors
of the helpless, yet again.
Isn't it cruel?
Blood.
Limbs.
Tears shake the ground.
Hopelessness.
Horror.
Absolute terror.
Seems like
we are never coming home.
The tears overflow.
The trees,
the sky,
the sea,
the ground
are weeping.
Killers of children,
what have you gained?
Is this who we are?
Oh,
what a shame
to have fallen
this far down.
Feels like a huge rock

has fallen
and another
and another.
We are stuck.

Home is not home anymore.
Home is a stranger,
a danger.
Home is screaming
for us to run away.
Pack your backs,
gather in boats,
and go!
Run away!
I said go!
Go
while you still have the chance
I am not safe anymore.

I am going to miss you.
I look back with tears in my eyes,
a heart heavy.

The corpses are scattered,
the dead neglected,
the little ones gazing aghast.
This is what you call trauma.
Now,
forever engraved in their hearts,
this is something they will never forget.
Home made me who I am.

587 deaths.
Doctors.
Students.
Children.
Mothers.
Fathers.
316 injuries.
The heart cannot be healed.

If you saw the scene,
you would be sleepless
for nights.
Somali u diida ceeb
Naftiina u diida cay

We're not clowns.
We're the entire circus.
Our enemies laughing at us
while we kill each other
Oo,
you hear that?
Smell that?
Feel the cold breeze?
Soo dhawoow Azrael
I am waiting for the day
all 5 of us are reunited
as one.
Ya Allah,
I will make Wudu
and call on you.
I will make salah;
I need you to say Amiin.

Dhiiga kuma dhaqaaqo miya?

The Quotidian Smiles, Smoke & Mirrors; But Am I there?
by Maqsud Hashi (age 18)

And so it begins,
the non-stop intrusive thoughts
that plague and enervate my being.
In my place
is the ghost
of the empty shell
I left.
Like a drowned rat,
I fight,
but I am spent.
I reach for my goals,
but this malediction
makes my mind weak.
But just like a dog with a bone,
I shall reach my peak.
And thus,
my cupidity to succeed
shall not wear off.
And so,
even in the face of this trickster,
I scoff.

Loud and Proud by Dio Rivera (age 20)

The sun gazes in my eyes,
time ticking by,
as I sit
and think why.
All the predicaments
and all the choices,
it's like a wave
that sways
its way
towards me.
But I can't shout,
too scared to be loud.
I'm not used to a crowd,
just sitting in fear
in a room
with the same air.
Nothing's fair
in this life,
people say
I say damn right.
I had to make my own way,
all my choices coming back
like a boomerang.
I said it once,
say it again,
it's just my luck.
They look down
when I approach,
aware of the art on my arms
They clutch their bags,
keeping alarm.
I'm seen as a threat
before seen as a person,
same struggles,
just a different story
and they ignore me.
They overlook my presence,
just a menace.

No real guidance
had me question my life
and my existence.
Now it's different.
When they sit
and listen,
makes them rethink
their thoughts
and now it's different.
Small circle
but I'm known to a lot,
not because of what I jot
or how I walk
and talk.
They know me
as the brown warrior
whose fought battles
bigger than any man can.
I'm known to my community
because I keep my brown fist raised
yelling,
"Si Se Puede!"
because I believe it,
because nobody else can.
I've kept it brown
and I was down
since a child.
From those Sunday night cruises on Federal
where it's known to get wild,
I'm not hiding.
I yell it proudly,
Chicano Power!
I get louder
on a mission to glory
with nobody to hold me,
just ignoring the stories.
Like a rose,
I keep growing.
Now I sit,
sun gazing in my eyes,

time ticking by,
no need to know why.
Scars big
but not seen,
not the type to perceive,
I just leave.
Fist raised,
making my own way,
breaking through walls
never fall,
I keep it tall.
I do it all.
As I walk
into the sunlit path
to success,
thinking about my ancestors
who know I'm the best.
Now,
I'm here,
still down
for the brown.
Always loud,
I say it proud:
Si Se Puede!
Yes We Can!

Made in United States
Troutdale, OR
10/07/2023

13468813R00066